FAMOUS BLIMPS AND AIRSHIPS

George Sullivan

Dodd, Mead & Company   **New York**

Other titles in this series

Famous Air Force Fighters
Famous Air Force Bombers
Famous Navy Fighter Planes
Famous Navy Attack Planes
Famous U.S. Spy Planes

PICTURE CREDITS

Goodyear Tire & Rubber Co., 1, 27, 37, 54, 55, 56, 62, 63; *Movie Star News*, 44, 45, 57; New York *Daily News*, 59; From the collection of Bill Sullivan, 7, 9, 32, 43; George Sullivan, 39, 60. All other photographs are from the Smithsonian Institution.

Published by Dodd, Mead & Company, Inc.,
71 Fifth Avenue, New York, N. Y. 10003

1 2 3 4 5 6 7 8 9 10

Library of Congress Cataloging-in-Publicaton Data

Sullivan, George, date
  Famous blimps and airships / George Sullivan.
    p.   cm.
  Summary: A history of dirigibles, describing the most famous of them, their accomplishments, and their fates.
  ISBN 0-396-09119-9
  1. Airships—Juvenile literature. [1. Airships.] I. Title.
TL650.S868 1988
629.133'24'09—dc19   87-32177
                                                  CIP
                                                  AC

The author is grateful to many people who helped him in the preparation of this book. Special thanks are due Lawrence E. Wilson, National Air and Space Museum; Anna Urband, Department of the Navy; David Miller and James Miller, Lighter-Than-Air Society; Richard F. Sailer, Goodyear Tire & Rubber Co.; Carol S. O'Loughlin, Fuji Photo Film U.S.A.; Capt. Trevor Hunt and Dana Kahn, Airship Industries; Carmen Matias, New York *Daily News*; Francesca Kurti, TLC Custom Labs; Madelyn Anderson and Bill Sullivan.

INTRODUCTION

They drift smoothly, lazily, seeming to ride invisible currents. There's something ghostlike about them. On the ground, every head tilts back to watch.

They're used mostly for advertising purposes today, or as airborne platforms for television cameras. But in the past, they were used in wartime as bombers and for protecting surface ships from submarines. In the 1930s, they carried passengers across oceans and continents, the way commercial jet planes do today.

They're airships—lighter-than-air aircraft. Each is made of a main body that contains helium, a lighter-than-air gas. The helium lifts the airship and keeps it in the air the same way a gas balloon (or toy balloon) is lifted. But airships are different from balloons because they have engines that move them through the air and equipment for steering.

Airships were introduced in the 1800s as the first manned flying machines. The fact that they could be controlled and steered led them to be called dirigibles. (The word "dirigible" comes from the Latin word *dirigere,* meaning "to direct.")

Dirigibles, or airships, are of two types: nonrigid and rigid. Nonrigid airships are the type flown today. They're usually called blimps.

The nonrigid airship consists mainly of a gasbag, or envelope, that contains the lifting gas. To make it easy for the gasbag to glide through the air, it's given a sausage shape. Its nose is stiffened by ribs that resemble the ribs in an umbrella.

There's a small cabin slung beneath the gasbag. The crew and passengers ride in the cabin, which is also called the control car or gondola. The bottom of the car rests on one or more landing wheels.

The car sometimes carries the airship's engines, its power plant, plus the engine fuel. Other times the engines are mounted inside the envelope.

The rigid airship is different. A masterpiece of structural engineering, the rigid airship is built like a skyscraper. Inside there's a metal frame. In the skyscraper, the outside walls and windows are hung on the frame. In the rigid airship, the lightweight metal framework is covered by a skin made of thin rubberized fabric.

Within the rigid airship's main structure,

called the hull, there are a number of compartments, or cells, that contain the lifting gas. The cabin is attached to the bottom of the hull.

Huge rigid airships were once used for regular passenger service between Europe and North and South America. By the late 1930s they were gone, however, replaced by passenger airplanes, which had become increasingly dependable. The spectacular crash of the *Hindenburg* in 1937 helped to hasten the close of the era of rigid airships.

As for nonrigids, their popularity keeps going up and down. In recent years, there has been a great revival of interest in them.

A blimp makes a perfect perch on which to mount TV cameras to shoot the action. A Goodyear blimp, for example, has performed this task at the World Series and Super Bowl and other major sports events. A dozen or so other companies have followed Goodyear's lead, and have begun using blimps as sky-going billboards.

The U.S. Navy is thinking of equipping airships with radar antennas that could cover a big expanse of ocean and detect low-flying enemy missiles. The U.S. Coast Guard is looking for an eye in the sky to help in search-and-rescue missions. A blimp could be just the thing.

As one observer put it, for airships, things are definitely looking up.

CONTENTS

LZ-1, completed in 1900, takes to the air over Lake Constance near Friedrichshafen in southern Germany.

LZ-1

Huge rigid airships, whose outer skin is supported by a framework of aluminum, were originally developed in Germany during the early 1900s. They were the work of a group of men inspired by Count Ferdinand von Zeppelin. Between the years 1900 and 1937, about 130 airships of this type were built and flown by Zeppelin's company.

The first of these zeppelins was built on a floating shed on Lake Constance, near Friedrichshafen, in southern Germany. It was designated the Luftschiff (air company) Zeppelin-1, or LZ-1.

Construction was completed in 1900. The airship was huge, 420 feet in length, more than twice as long as a Goodyear blimp of the present day. Since the LZ-1's diameter was almost 8-feet less than that of a blimp, the airship had a much slimmer appearance.

The LZ-1 took to the air for the first time on July 2, 1900. It was a shaky performance. With a crew of five aboard, the airship climbed nervously to about 1,000 feet over Lake Constance to make an 18-minute flight of three and a half miles. Earlier airships had flown farther and faster.

It was obvious that the LZ-1 lacked both power and stability. The ship's rudders were too tiny to be of any use. But the crew did manage to bring the airship to a safe landing on the surface of the lake. The day after the flight, a Frankfurt newspaper noted that the Count's experiments, while "extremely interesting, have undoubtedly proved conclusively that a dirigible balloon is of practically no value."

Such criticism didn't stop the Count. He continued to tinker with the LZ-1. In October, 1900, he made two more flights in the airship. On one, he stayed aloft for an hour and a half. On the other, he got the airship's speed up to 17 miles an hour.

More sophisticated airships followed in the wake of the LZ-1. Von Zeppelin's LZ-3 made long flights over southern Germany in 1909.

The LZ-10, completed in 1911 and named the

Schwaben, made its first flight on July 20 of that year, traveling from Friedrichshafen to Lucerne in central Switzerland. For the next eleven months, the *Schwaben* toiled in passenger service, making a total of 218 flights, carrying 1,553 passengers. The airship was wrecked in a gale-force wind in June, 1912.

In the years that followed, other of von Zeppelin's airships continued to make passenger flights over mapped routes. More than 10,000 fare-paying customers were carried. Not one of them suffered so much as a scratch.

Von Zeppelin was honored in an uncommon way. Jules Leotard, who popularized the snugly fitting elastic garment worn by dancers and gymnasts, and Rudolf Diesel, inventor of a unique type of engine, earned similar honors. Their names became part of the English language. Today, the word zeppelin means any rigid airship with a long cylinder-shaped body.

Other Data (LZ-1)
Length: 420 ft.
Diameter: 38.2 ft.
Gas Volume: 399,000 cu. ft.
Power Plant: Two 14.7 hp Daimler engines
Maximum Speed: 17.3 mph

Advertisement in *Scientific American* for October 14, 1911, offered readers "Daily Passenger Trips by Zeppelin-Airship."

During World War I, German zeppelins such as this one made fifty bombing raids on England, killing hundreds and causing widespread damage.

LZ-38

Beginning in 1914, zeppelins began carrying bombs instead of passengers. World War I was the reason.

The war was fought mainly in Europe and the Middle East. It pitted the Allies, chiefly Great Britain, France, and Russia, against the Central Powers, Germany and Austria-Hungary. The war ended in 1918 with the collapse of the Central Powers.

The huge airships were a dramatic new weapon in World War I. The Zeppelin Company agreed to build new airships by the dozens for the German army and navy. The British also flew airships during the war, eight of them. But from a technical standpoint, they were several years behind the German airships, and never had much impact.

Germany's army used von Zeppelin's airships to raid cities in Belgium, France, Poland, Romania, and Russia. But England was Germany's main target.

Airship raids were always made at night and usually during the dark of the moon, that period extending eight days before the new moon to eight days after it. During that phase, the airships were least visible to the British fighter planes and antiaircraft gunners.

At first, the airships were permitted to bomb only docks and military installations along the English coast and on the lower Thames River. The city of London was not a target.

This policy changed early in May, 1915. Permission was given to bomb the British capital, although the attacks had to be limited to the military targets that fringed the city.

The LZ-38, an army airship piloted by Captain Erich Linnarz, was the first zeppelin to drop bombs on London. The raid took place on the night of May 31, 1915. "London was all lit up and we enjoyed total surprise," Linnarz wrote in his report. "Not a searchlight or an antiaircraft gun was aimed at us before the first bomb was dropped."

The LZ-38 stayed over the British capital for about ten minutes. The 154 bombs the ship released killed seven people and injured 35. The bombs also started dozens of fires.

The LZ-38 had a very short life. A week after its attack on London, two British aircraft bombed the airship in its hangar near Brussels, Belgium. Although the bombs were tiny, weighing only 20 pounds, they were enough to ignite the airship's hydrogen gas, reducing the LZ-38 to ashes in a matter of minutes.

Between January, 1915, and August, 1918, German airships made a total of fifty raids on Britain. The nearly 200 tons of bombs they dropped killed hundreds and caused millions of dollars in damage.

But most of the damage was done early in the war, when the airships were able to roam freely without fear of British guns. The British eventually turned the tide, inflicting heavy losses on Germany's airship fleets. The German navy lost 53 of its 73 airships to British fighter planes and antiaircraft fire. Four of every ten crewmen died. For the army, casualties were not quite so heavy, but of its 50 airships, the German army lost 26.

Count Ferdinand von Zeppelin died in 1917, a year before the war ended. He never lived to see the defeat of Germany—nor the days of zeppelin glory that followed the war.

Other Data (LZ-38)
Length: 536 ft.
Diameter: 61 ft.
Gas Volume: 1,126,000 cu. ft.
Power Plant: Four 210 hp Maybach engines
Maximum Speed: 60 mph

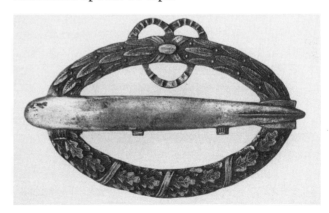

Badge worn by World War I German army zeppelin pilots.

B-SERIES

The U.S. Navy first became interested in airships in 1916. The British had reported that nonrigids had operated successfully against German submarines during World War I, and it was this type of airship with which the Americans began to experiment.

The Navy called their nonrigids "blimps," a word the British had invented. In an attempt to distinguish their nonrigids from the rigid airships the Germans were flying, the British called their nonrigids "Limps." The first category of Limps became known as "A-Limps." The second category was called "B-Limps." Out of that, the word "blimp" was born.

Early in 1917, when it began to appear that the United States was going to be drawn into World War I, the Navy ordered sixteen blimps from the Goodyear Tire & Rubber Co. of Akron, Ohio. These nonrigids, which were included in a "B-Series," were intended for use against German submarines.

The United States entered World War I on April 6, 1917, with a declaration of war against Germany. Just a few weeks later, the first American airship intended for wartime operations was tested. The ship made several test flights, including one that lasted twelve hours. Meanwhile, construction was moving ahead on the other ships the Navy had ordered and 600 volunteers for the

In B-Series blimps, control car was suspended from the airbag by cables.

Navy's airship service began training.

During the summer of 1918, Germany stepped up submarine activity off the East Coast of the United States. Six submarines destroyed 100 boats and ships, killing 435 people.

Most of the vessels sent to the bottom were

10

fishing boats, tankers, or merchant ships. But the total also included the cruiser *San Diego*, which was sunk by a mine, an explosive device that had been placed in the water by a submarine. The mine exploded when struck by the cruiser. The sinking took place off Fire Island, New York.

Airships were the Navy's chief weapon in the struggle against the German submarine menace. Operating from air stations that had been established at Chatham on Cape Cod, Massachusetts; Montauk and Rockaway on Long Island, New York; Cape May, New Jersey; Norfolk, Virginia; and Key West, Florida, B-Series airships put in some 13,600 hours in the air and covered over 400,000 miles on patrol duty. Although they were designed to stay aloft for no more than 16 hours, some of the blimps logged flights as long as 40 hours.

On at least two occasions, B-class airships sighted and bombed enemy submarines. Another time, an airship drove off a sub that was attempting to lay mines in the shipping lanes just outside of New York Harbor.

Not long before World War I ended, the Navy ordered an advanced airship from Goodyear. Known as the C-type, these blimps boasted several improvements over B-Series airships, including twin engines that made for a top speed of 60 miles per hour. (B-class craft traveled at a maximum speed of 45 miles an hour.)

The first airship in the C-Series was suc-cessfully flown in September, 1918. Not long after, World War I ended. C-class blimps that were delivered to the Navy through the remaining months of 1918 and in the years that followed wrote an important chapter in the history of non-rigids. Nevertheless, those of the B-Series rank as the first successful military airships developed by the United States.

Other Data (B-1 - B-9)
Length: 160 ft.
Diameter: 31.5 ft.
Gas Volume: 77,000 cu. ft.
Power Plant: One 100 hp Curtiss OXX-2 engine
Maximum Speed: 45 mph

Goodyear produced sixteen B-Series blimps for the U.S. Navy. They saw service during World War I.

C-SERIES

The C-1, the first in the C-Series of nonrigid airships, was successfully flown for the first time in September, 1918. This airship, and the other nine in the series ordered by the Navy, were intended for antisubmarine duty during World War I. But the war ended on November 11, 1918. Thus, C-class airships never saw active duty. Nevertheless, they still accomplished a great deal.

The C-class ship carried a crew of four. The men were housed in a control car that resembled the fuselage of an airplane and was attached to the airbag by long cables.

Two pusher-type engines powered the airship. One engine was mounted on each side of the control car.

The control car was built by a division of the Curtiss Aeroplane and Motor Company. Two other companies were responsible for the manufacture of the airship itself. Goodyear built the C-1, C-3, C-4, C-5, C-7, and C-8. Goodrich turned out the C-2, C-6, C-9, and C-10.

On December 12, 1918, the C-1 hauled a Curtiss JN-4 biplane to an altitude of 2,500 feet, then released it, the pilot gliding the aircraft safely to earth. It marked the first time this experiment had been safely conducted in the U.S. In the future, airships would house small airplanes, retrieving and launching them. The test con-

ducted by the C-1 showed that such operations were possible.

In February, 1919, the C-3, while hovering over a surface ship at sea, was successfully refueled from the vessel.

The C-2 and C-4 were turned over to the U.S. Army in 1921. In 1922, while being operated by the Army, the C-2 completed the first nonstop air crossing of the United States by an airship. The voyage began at Langley Field, Virginia, and ended at Arcadia, California.

The C-7, on December 1, 1921, became the first airship in the world to fly with helium instead of hydrogen as the lifting gas. After the successful test, helium, which does not have the explosive properties of hydrogen, was ordered for all U.S. military airships. In addition, the Navy was given control of all the nation's natural gas wells. (Helium is derived from natural gas.)

The C-5 had a chance to become better known than any of the other blimps in the C-Series. It was planned that the C-5 would become the first airship to cross the Atlantic Ocean.

On May 14, 1919, the C-5 took to the air from its base at Montauk on the eastern tip of Long Island and headed north and east for St. John's, Newfoundland, a distance of 1,022 miles, the first leg of the voyage to Europe. The cruiser *Chicago* had

Control car for C-class blimps resembled the fuselage of an airplane.

12

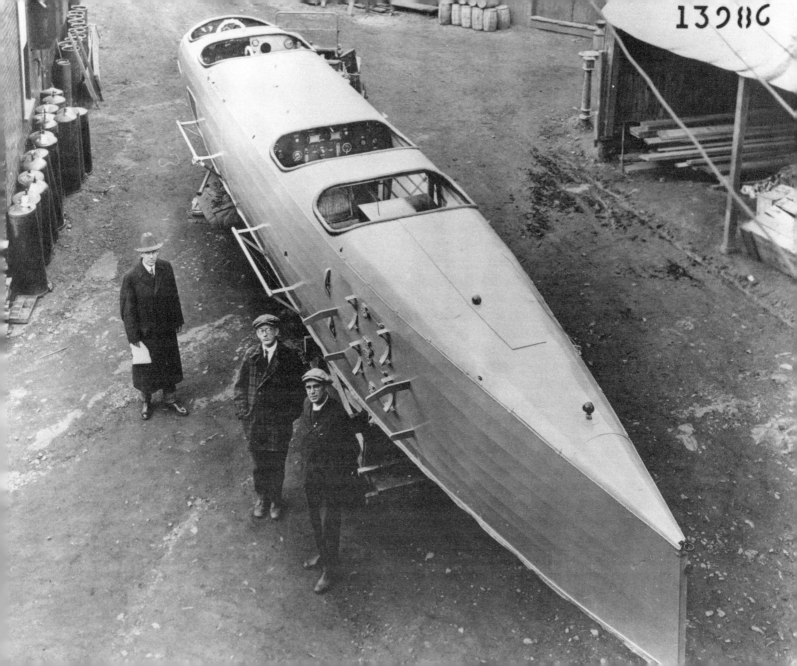

gone ahead to St. John's. Men from the ship were sent ashore to serve as a ground crew at a makeshift base the C-5 was to use.

Cruising at an average speed of nearly 60 miles an hour, the C-5 made the trip to St. John's in slightly more than 24 hours. There the airship was refueled. Food was put aboard. Mechanics from the *Chicago* fine-tuned the engines.

On the morning of May 16, 1919, as the C-5 crew was resting aboard the *Chicago* before the final hop, a fierce wind began to blow. The ground crew, manning ropes, sought to keep the ship from being swept out to sea. Some of the men were dragged over the rocky ground. More sailors were put on the lines.

The wind kept getting stronger. It slammed the airship to the ground, damaging one of the engines. Then it picked the ship up again.

By this time, the airship's crew was on the scene. Two of the men started climbing up the

C-5 made a valiant attempt to be the first airship to cross the Atlantic Ocean.

Dating to 1918, highly successful C-Series blimps achieved many historic firsts.

cables leading from the cabin to the airbag. Their plan was to slash the airbag, releasing the hydrogen. The airship would then fall to the ground, where it could be controlled. Later the slashes would be repaired and the hydrogen replaced.

But before the two men could carry out the plan, a violent gust caught the ship and lifted it still higher and out of the grasp of the ground crew. The men climbing the cables fell to the ground. One broke an ankle in the fall.

The crewless airship surged out over the Atlantic. The ground crew watched helplessly as it became a speck in the eastern sky and then disappeared. The C-5 was never seen again.

Within a week, the NC-4, a big Navy flying boat, completed a flight from Newfoundland to Portugal, with a stop in the Azores for fuel. The flight marked the first time the Atlantic had been crossed in the air.

And early in July, 1919, Great Britain's R-34, a huge rigid, became the first airship to make the Atlantic crossing. But a tiny blimp came close to capturing both honors.

Other Data (C-1 - C-10)
Length: 192 ft.
Diameter: 42 ft.
Gas Volume: 181,000 cu. ft.
Power Plant: Two 200-hp Hall-Scott L-6 Pusher-
    type engines
Maximum Speed: 60 mph

In 1919, R-34 attempted the first east-to-west aerial crossing of the Atlantic Ocean—and succeeded.

R-34

It was September, 1916. World War I raged in Europe. A German naval zeppelin, the L-33, was sent to bomb England. When it arrived over British soil, fighter planes took to the air. The gunfire from one opened holes in the ship's airbag and it began sinking toward the ground. It eventually came down in a field near Little Wigborough in Essex.

In the weeks that followed, the British studied the wreckage carefully. Using the L-33 as a model, they built two rigids, the R-33 and R-34. They were two of the best airships of the time.

Both ships were launched in March, 1919. Since World War I had ended by that time, plans were made to put them into commercial service, carrying passengers between England and perhaps Egypt and India.

Before that happened, however, the R-34 was ordered to prepare for a transatlantic crossing. The Atlantic was to be crossed twice by airplane in the spring of 1919, both times from west to east, from North America to Europe. But no aircraft had ever tried to buck the stiff headwinds of an east-to-west flight.

That was the R-34's ambition as it lifted from its base in East Fortune, Scotland, on July 2, 1919. Major George Herbert Scott commanded a crew of thirty. Also aboard was a kitten and a stowaway, an unauthorized passenger by the name of William Ballantyne, who hid himself in the hull, making his appearance after the ship had been aloft for about twelve hours and was over the ocean. If the R-34 had been over land, Ballantyne would have been ordered to parachute down. But now there was no choice but to take him to America.

Although the airship traveled in thick clouds for most of the journey, the trip was uneventful. Heavy rain clouds were encountered early in the evening of the second day, but the R-34 was able to climb above them with ease.

There was excitement toward the end of the journey as fuel became a problem. Major Scott began to doubt whether the ship had enough fuel to reach its destination, Roosevelt Field at Mineola, Long Island. As a precaution, Scott radioed Chatham, Massachusetts, and told the base there to prepare for an emergency landing.

But before long, the winds turned favorable and helped to carry the R-34 toward New York. As the R-34 arrived over Roosevelt Field, one of the airship's crew members, Major J. E. M. Pritchard, jumped from the airship by parachute to supervise the landing.

The R-34 had made the first east-to-west crossing of the Atlantic by air in 108 hours, 12 minutes. It also had another "first" to its credit. In William Ballantyne, the airship had the first transatlantic stowaway.

Three days later, the R-34 made the return trip to England, setting down at Pulham after a flight of 75 hours, 2 minutes. It thus became the first aircraft to make a round trip over the Atlantic.

Other Data (R-34)
Length: 643 ft.
Diameter: 89 ft.
Gas Volume: 1,950,000
Power Plant: Five 275-hp Sunbeam engines
Maximum Speed: 55 mph

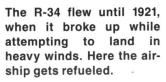

The R-34 flew until 1921, when it broke up while attempting to land in heavy winds. Here the airship gets refueled.

ZR-1 *SHENANDOAH*

The success of German rigid airships before, during, and after World War I awakened the interest of the U.S. Navy. Navy experts believed that zeppelins could be valuable in scouting missions, particularly in the vast Pacific, where American bases were few in number with enormous distances between them.

In 1919, Congress voted funds for the construction of two giant rigids. One of the airships, designated the ZR-1, was to be built in the United States. (The Z stood for zeppelin; the R, for rigid.) The other ship was to be built by the British, who were to call it the R-38. To the U.S. Navy, however, it was the ZR-2.

The ZR-2 never got a chance to prove itself. During a test flight in the summer of 1921, the ship broke apart and exploded, an accident that resulted in the death of 16 Americans and 28 Britons.

Despite this disaster, the Navy gave no thought of abandoning work on the ZR-1. Eventually it would be named the *Shenandoah*. (An Indian name, Shenandoah has been translated as "daughter of the stars.")

Parts for the *Shenandoah* were manufactured at the Naval Aircraft factory at the Philadelphia Navy Yard. They were then trucked to the Naval Air Station at Lakehurst, New Jersey, where the only hangar big enough to hold the completed airship was to be found. There the *Shenandoah* was assembled.

The *Shenandoah* was the first rigid airship to be inflated with helium, a rare gas that had first been isolated in 1895. Although it weighs a bit more than hydrogen and does not have quite the lifting ability, helium is, unlike hydrogen, non-flammable. Its use in an airship practically guarantees no fire aloft. (The R-38 had used hydrogen.)

Manned by a crew of 23, the *Shenandoah* made its first flight on September 4, 1923. The airship did not perform as well as everyone hoped it would. It had been originally designed to use hydrogen as a lifting gas. In changing over to helium, several valves important to the maneuvering of the airship had to be removed.

Despite the problems, the Navy had big plans for the *Shenandoah*. A flight over the North Pole was mapped out. Only once had the North Pole been reached up to that time, and that was by a land expedition led by Admiral Robert E. Peary in 1909. The Pole was beyond the range of any airplane of the day.

But before the *Shenandoah* was able to embark on its Polar flight, the airship was damaged when blown from its mooring mast in a storm. It was the

The *Shenandoah* was assembled at U.S. Navy's huge hangar at Lakehurst, New Jersey.

Called a "battleship of the sky," the U.S. Navy's *Shenandoah* made its first flight on September 4, 1923.

Shenandoah was the first zeppelin to moor to a floating mast. Ship is the tanker *Patoka*.

first of a number of accidents that the airship was to suffer.

The next time the *Shenandoah* flew was in 1924. The flight took the airship on a 9,317-mile journey back and forth across the United States, with stopovers for fuel at Fort Worth, Texas; San Diego, California; and Seattle, Washington.

Everywhere the *Shenandoah* went, huge crowds turned out to gaze in wonder. The flight was said to represent a giant step forward in the development of commercial passenger service by airship.

In spite of this success, plans to send the *Shenandoah* to the North Pole were scrapped. Instead, the ship made dozens of other flights, 57 in all.

The last one was fatal. On September 2, 1925, the *Shenandoah* cast off from Lakehurst with 43 men aboard. St. Louis, Missouri, was the airship's destination. Visits to Minneapolis and Detroit were also planned.

Very early the next day, while over the town of Caldwell, Ohio, the *Shenandoah* ran into violent storms. Brilliant flashes of lightning filled the sky. Gale-force winds slammed into the airship, tossing it first in one direction, then another.

At one point, turbulent air currents forced the nose of the ship up and up until it was almost pointing toward the sky. At the same time, shrieking winds hammered at the hull. The huge airship shuddered. Then, with the tremendous roar of wrenching metal, the airship broke into three pieces.

Two sections of the *Shenandoah* crashed to earth, killing 14 crewmen. But a third section was brought down safely through the skill of one of the ship's officers, who maneuvered the fragment as if it were a free balloon. The section landed in a cornfield.

Twenty-nine crewmen managed to survive the disaster. Had the *Shenandoah* been inflated with explosive hydrogen, not helium, it is likely that no one would have survived.

In the days that followed, swarms of the curious flocked to eastern Ohio where the sections of the wreckage of the *Shenandoah* had come down. They picked over the rubble in search of souvenirs. A tailor in Marietta, Ohio, claimed parts of the airship's rubberized gasbags. He turned them into raincoats that he called "Shenandoah Slickers."

Other Data (ZR-1 *Shenandoah*)
Length: 680 ft.
Diameter: 79 ft.
Gas Volume: 2,115,000 cu. ft.
Power Plant: Six 300-hp Packard engines
Maximum Speed: 60 mph

The *Shenandoah* tragedy caused big headlines, not only in Ohio but throughout the United States.

ZR-3 *LOS ANGELES*

Of all the zeppelins the U.S. Navy operated during the 1920s and 1930s, none was as successful as the *Los Angeles*. The airship made more than 300 successful flights and carried out many experimental missions with the fleet.

The *Los Angeles* was German-built. After Germany was defeated in World War I, an inter-Allied reparations commission was formed to decide how Germany should pay for the damages and losses the victorious nations had suffered

The *Los Angeles*, the U.S. Navy's most successful airship, soars above the Washington Monument.

during the war. The commission decided that the United States should receive $800,000 in gold. Instead of paying that amount, Germany offered to build the U.S. Navy a zeppelin with a gas capacity of some 2,500,000 cubic feet.

Once approval was given, the Zeppelin Company set to work. The airship was designated LZ-126 by the Germans. To the Americans it was ZR-3.

Count Hugo Eckener himself, the operational chief of the Zeppelin Company, and who had come to be regarded as the world's leading expert on lighter-than-air aircraft, was to pilot the completed airship from the factory at Friedrichshafen to the Naval Air Station at Lakehurst.

The giant airship arrived over the eastern shore of the United States early in the morning of October 16, 1924. Naval officials at Lakehurst learned of the ship's presence at 3:15 A.M. when they received a radio message saying: "Cape Cod light on port beam. Speed 32 knots. Headed for Boston."

About an hour later, early morning risers in Boston scanned the still dark sky for a glimpse of the big airship, which passed over the city at an altitude of only 1,000 feet. Its lights flashed clearly.

South-southwest of Boston, farmers occupied with morning chores heard the airship's engines, then looked up to see the silvery shape. The ZR-3 then soared over Providence, Rhode Island, New-

Using a trapezelike device, the *Los Angeles* experiments in snaring an airplane out of the sky.

port, and Westerly, and past New London, Connecticut. By now, the sun had brightened the morning sky. "We will land about nine or ten o'clock," the airship radioed the base at Lakehurst.

At 6:30 A.M., the airship cruised past New Haven, Connecticut, then Bridgeport. At 7:10 A.M. over Mitchel Field near Mineola, New York, the airship was joined in the sky by four small Army planes.

Over New York, the airship created a sensation. It dipped down and down toward the towering skyscrapers clustered at the southern tip of Manhattan Island until it seemed it would touch their tips. Factory whistles saluted the airship. Ships in the harbor and at the docks that ringed the city also sounded greetings. Cries of "There she is!" went up from the streets as hundreds pointed to the sky.

The huge ship headed directly north over the center of the city, veered toward New Jersey, then circled back over the Bronx and back down over Manhattan a second time. Thousands of work-bound New Yorkers halted in the streets to gape. Thousands of others, when they heard the drumming sound of the approaching engines, rushed to their apartment windows or hurried to the rooftops or out onto the streets. Many had overcoats draped over pajamas.

At one downtown intersection, people watching filled the street from curb to curb, halting

traffic. On Ellis Island in New York Harbor, hundreds of immigrants were awed by the sight of the zeppelin against the background of the city's skyline.

Shortly before 10:00 A.M., the airship arrived at Lakehurst. When President Calvin Coolidge learned that the ZR-3 was safely down, he sent a telegram to Eckener congratulating him on the "skill and efficiency of the German technicians." Not long after the airship's arrival, it was named the *Los Angeles.*

For its delivery flight from Germany, the *Los Angeles* had been filled with hydrogen. Helium was scarce and very expensive in those days. But the U.S. Navy had no wish to operate the *Los Angeles* with hazardous hydrogen. The only helium available was contained in the *Shenandoah,* which was also berthed at Lakehurst. So the *Los Angeles* was drained of its hydrogen, and then the helium from the *Shenandoah* was pumped into it. Not until 1925 was there enough helium available to allow both the *Los Angeles* and *Shenandoah* to operate at the same time.

In its many years of service, the *Los Angeles* made 331 flights and accumulated 5,368 hours in the air. It journeyed to Panama and Cuba. It con-

An alert photographer snapped this picture as the *Los Angeles,* lifted by a gust of wind, stands on its nose at its mooring mast in Lakehurst, New Jersey. Airship returned gently to a normal position.

ducted experiments in retrieving small aircraft by means of a specially designed trapeze that hung from the airship's underside. It landed and took off from the flight deck of the carrier *Saratoga*.

The *Los Angeles* was taken out of service in 1932, but it remained in retirement for only a year. After the *Akron* was lost at sea in 1933 (page 39), the *Los Angeles* was put back into commission. It saw only limited use in the years that followed, however. In 1940, when it was finally scrapped, the *Los Angeles* had managed to last longer than any other Navy rigid airship.

Other Data (ZR-3 *Los Angeles*)
Length: 658 ft.
Diameter: 90.6 ft.
Gas Volume: 2,472,000 cu. ft.
Power Plant: Five 400-hp Maybach engines
Maximum Speed: 76 mph

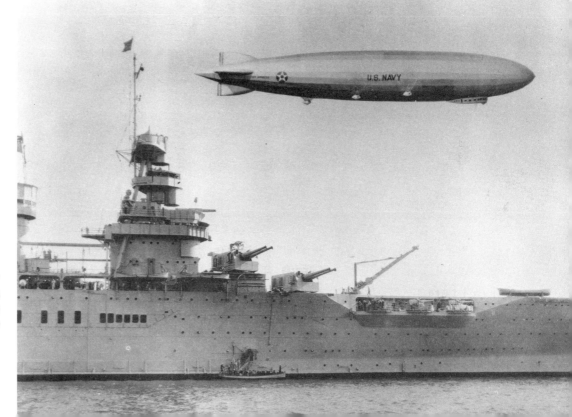

The "pride of the Navy" the *Los Angeles* was called. Here the airship operates with units of the fleet.

GOODYEAR *PILGRIM*

During the mid-1920s, U.S. Navy experts in lighter-than-air aircraft focused their attention on rigids, on the *Shenandoah* and *Los Angeles*. These giant zeppelins were what excited the general public, too.

But the Goodyear Company saw a need for much smaller, nonrigid airships. In 1925, Goodyear began building a fleet of nonrigids to be used for advertising purposes and training airship crew members. The *Pilgrim*, which was test-flown in June, 1925, was the first of these commercial blimps to be completed by Goodyear.

The *Pilgrim* was the first blimp to use several design features that would be included in all future commercial and military nonrigids.

For example, the control car for the helium-inflated *Pilgrim*, made of steel tubing that was covered with magnesium sheeting, was fastened directly to the envelope. In all previous blimps, the cabin had been suspended from the envelope by cables. The control car had room enough for four people—the pilot, a mechanic, and two passengers.

The *Pilgrim* had four hinged tail fins to help control it. The two mounted at the top and bottom, used to turn the ship to the right or left, were the craft's rudders. The two fins mounted at the sides, known as elevators, were used in ascending and descending. The advanced design of the *Pilgrim*'s elevators and rudders influenced fin construction for decades.

The *Pilgrim* went into active service in July, 1925, and remained in operation until December 30, 1931, when it was retired. By that time, the *Pilgrim* had made 4,765 flights, carried 5,355 passengers, and flown 94,474 miles.

A pilgrim, says the dictionary, is a wanderer or traveler. The *Pilgrim* blimp was well named.

The *Pilgrim* was followed in 1928 by Goodyear's *Puritan*. The *Volunteer, Mayflower, Vigilant*, and the 179,000 cubic-foot *Defender* came in 1929. The *Reliance, Resolute, Rainbow*, and *Ranger* were noted Goodyear blimps of the 1930s. All drew upon design and construction features pioneered by the *Pilgrim*.

Other Data (Pilgrim)
Length: 105.5 ft.
Diameter: 31 ft.
Gas Volume: 47,700 cu. ft.
Power Plant: One 60 hp Lawrence L-4 engine
Maximum Speed: 40 mph

Launched in 1925, *Pilgrim* was the first of the Goodyear Company's advertising blimps.

NORGE

Norwegian explorer Roald Amundsen who, in 1911, had been the first man to reach the South Pole, failed in 1923 in an attempt to fly over the North Pole in an airplane. He tried again in 1925 and failed again.

In 1926, he made the attempt a third time. For this try, the fifty-three-year-old Amundsen relied on an airship he had purchased from the Italian government. He christened the airship the *Norge* (the Norwegian name of Norway) and placed it under the command of its Italian designer, Umberto Nobile.

On April 10, 1926, the *Norge* took off from Rome on the first leg of its long voyage. Nobile zigzagged his way north, stopping at Pulham in England; Oslo, Norway; and Leningrad, Russia. There the flight expedition was delayed three weeks before weather conditions permitted the ship to continue to Vadsø on the northern tip of Norway, and from there to Kings Bay in Spitzbergen, one of a group of islands in the Arctic Ocean north of Norway.

At Kings Bay, final preparations for the Polar flight were made. The airship's engines were overhauled and its fuel tanks and hydrogen cells were filled to capacity.

By the morning of May 11, 1926, everything was ready. The *Norge* lifted into the sky from the snow of Kings Bay and headed for the Pole. Its sixteen crewmen included eight Norwegians, six Italians, one Swede, and one American.

The airship cruised steadily at an altitude of 1,350 feet over the frozen Arctic Ocean at a speed of about 50 miles an hour. It was the time of year when the Arctic day is close to 24 hours in length. But although the sun shone constantly, it was freezing cold inside the control car. The metal parts of the airship outside the cabin became caked with ice. Ice even began to form inside the control car.

Not quite 350-feet in length and capable of a maximum speed of 70 miles an hour, Italian-built *Norge* carried sixteen passengers across the North Pole.

The ship encountered patches of thick fog from time to time but these caused no problem. The *Norge* held steadily on its course.

At 1:20 A.M. on May 12, the navigator made the final calculations that would bring the *Norge* directly over the Pole. Amundsen and members of the crew stood by to drop Norwegian, Italian, and American flags. Suddenly the navigator called out, "Ready with the flags!" A moment later, he cried, "Now, we're here!"

Down the flags fluttered, the Norwegian flag first. It landed upright, standing in the snow on its aluminum shaft.

Instead of turning about and returning to Kings Bay, Nobile headed the *Norge* directly across the earth's summit with Nome, Alaska, as his destination. The weather grew steadily worse. Ice formed on the airship's propellers, then flew off as the propellers spun. The flying chunks of ice ripped holes in the lower part of the envelope. The crew was able to repair the worst of the damage, however.

Early on the morning of May 13, the navigator cried: "Land ahead to starboard!" It was the coast of Alaska. A few hours later, the airship passed over the small Alaskan village of Wainwright.

The explorers were the first to fly an airship over the North Pole and the first to cross the Arctic from one edge to the other. In their long, bitter-cold journey, they had seen nothing but frozen water.

After its North Pole voyage, *Norge* did not fly again. Here ground crewmen help to land the airship safely.

Other Data (Norge)
Length: 347 ft.
Diameter: 63 ft.
Gas Volume: 654,000 cu. ft.
Power Plant: Three 250-hp Maybach engines
Maximum Speed: 70 mph

ZMC-2

It was one of the world's most unusual airships. Called the "Tin Balloon," it was neither a rigid airship or a blimp. Designed in the early 1920s and built during the final years of the decade, the ZMC-2 had an outer skin made of thin strips of aluminum, each less than 1/16 of an inch in thickness, that were riveted together. It was the world's first all-metal airship.

The ZMC-2 was built by the Aircraft Development Corporation of Detroit, Michigan. More than 3.5 million rivets were used in its construction. In order to deal with that many rivets, the company developed an automatic riveter that was capable of inserting over 5,000 rivets an hour. Even so, it took more than a year to build the ZMC-2.

The airship was delivered to the Navy on September 12, 1929. It was called a ZMC—for Zep-

First flown on August 19, 1929, the aluminum-skinned ZMC-2 was one of the most unusual airships ever built.

pelin, Metal-Clad. Final tests were completed before the end of the month.

About the same size as one of Goodyear's advertising blimps of the 1980s, the ZMC-2, unlike a fabric blimp, had no tendency to sag or crumple when the air pressure inside the envelope was reduced. Like a big metal egg, the ZMC-2 always held its shape.

But the ZMC-2 had a failing that no one anticipated. When the blimp ascended and the air pressure increased, causing contraction of the helium, small ridges or furrows developed in the thin metal envelope. In other words, the ZMC-2 had a skin that wrinkled.

Another shortcoming was the bumpy ride that passengers sometimes got. This caused airsickness, which did not make the ZMC-2 popular with members of its crew.

The ZMC-2 served with the Navy until 1935. Then the airship was deflated and inspected from stem to stern. The metal hull was found to be in topflight condition, except for some wrinkles.

After being reinflated, the Tin Bubble continued on active duty until 1939. By that time, it had been in service for ten years, a very long life by airship standards. It made a total of 751 flights.

During the early 1940s, Navy funds meant for blimp construction went toward the building of nonrigids, that is, fabric-covered airships. Metalclads weren't considered. The ZMC-2 turned out to be one of a kind.

Other Data (ZMC-2)
Length: 149 ft.
Diameter: 52 ft.
Gas Volume: 202,000 cu. ft.
Power Plant: Two 220-hp Wright Whirlwind
     engines
Maximum Speed: 70 mph

Final flight of the ZMC-2 took place on August 19, 1939, exactly ten years after its first flight.

LZ-127 *GRAF ZEPPELIN*

Germany's *Graf Zeppelin*, officially known as the LZ-127, launched at Friedrichshafen in 1928, was the most successful airship ever built. Between the years 1928 and 1937, it flew over a million miles in commercial service, carrying over 13,000 passengers.

At the time the *Graf Zeppelin* was built, it was the world's biggest airship, stretching 776 feet in length and with a diameter of 100 feet. And with the ability to cruise at a speed of 80 miles an hour, it was also the world's fastest.

The airship was named for Count Ferdinand von Zeppelin, Germany's airship pioneer, who had died in 1917. (*Graf* is the German word for count.)

The *Graf Zeppelin's* first flight took place on September 18, 1928. Everything worked perfectly. Afterward, *Time* magazine noted: "Certainly for transoceanic trips, the airship is the thing."

Virtually every person who crossed the Atlantic in those days did so by passenger liner. It was risky business to attempt to make the crossing in an airplane.

Passengers aboard the *Graf Zeppelin* were offered many of the same luxuries one would expect to find aboard a fine ship. The airship's control car, nearly 100 feet long and 20 feet wide,

Some of the thousands on hand to greet the *Graf Zeppelin* on its visit to London.

was fitted out with a handsome lounge that converted into a dining room at mealtime. The room had heavy wine-red drapes and thick carpeting.

Professional chefs staffed the galley. Though small, it produced excellent meals. Table settings included silverware, elegant crystal, and fine china.

On the morning of October 11, 1928, the *Graf Zeppelin* left Friedrichshafen for Lakehurst, New Jersey. Aboard were a crew of 40 and 20 passengers.

When the great ship landed safely at Lakehurst 111 hours and 42 minutes later, a crowd of over 20,000 cheered loudly. Hugo Eckener, who commanded the flight, and the members of his crew were honored with a ticker-tape parade up New York's Broadway and were guests of President Calvin Coolidge at the White House.

In the months that followed, Eckener made one spectacular flight after another in an effort to keep the *Graf Zeppelin* in the public eye. In March, 1929, the airship left the freezing temperatures of western Europe for a three-day, 5,000-mile cruise in the sun. Passengers were treated to stunning views of the French Riviera, Mount Vesuvius in Italy, Naples, and Rome. They drifted by moonlight over the Dead Sea. A month

The *Graf Zeppelin* cruises over the tip of Manhattan Island in New York City.

The *Graf Zeppelin* carried 20 passengers and a crew of 40. Here crew members pose with the giant airship.

later, Eckener and the airship made a similar voyage over Spain and Portugal.

By mid-1929, Eckener was planning his most ambitious project—a flight around the world. Such a flight had been made by airplane in 1924. But that journey had taken 175 days and involved more stops than anyone could count. Eckener planned to make the trip with only three stops, while carrying a normal load of crew, passengers, and freight.

Amid a great wave of publicity, the *Graf Zeppelin* left Lakehurst early on August 8, 1929, bound for Friedrichshafen, the first stop. Five days later, the airship departed for Tokyo, a flight that took it over desolate stretches of the Soviet Union where no aircraft had ever flown.

In Tokyo, the Japanese gave the airship's passengers and crew an extraordinary welcome, honoring the travelers for four full days with banquets, speeches, and gifts.

Then it was across the Pacific to the West Coast of the United States. The zeppelin arrived over San Francisco, then headed south to Los Angeles, where it stopped briefly before crossing the continent to Lakehurst. The airship arrived there on August 29. The 'round-the-world voyage had been completed in 21 days, 7 hours, and 34 minutes.

The parade up Broadway honoring Eckener and his crew was one of the biggest in history. At a White House reception, the new President, Herbert Hoover, declared: "I thought the days of the great explorers like Magellan and Columbus had passed. But now I see another great explorer, Dr. Hugo Eckener, standing before me."

In the years that followed, the *Graf Zeppelin* pioneered regular commercial air service between Germany and South America. A dozen or so flights were scheduled each year from 1932 through 1935. The service was extremely popular among the large German-speaking population of Brazil.

In 1933, the *Graf Zeppelin* completed its 380th flight. It had crossed the Atlantic Ocean 51 times and had logged more than half a million miles.

The *Graf Zeppelin* continued in service until 1937. In May of that year, Germany's *Hindenburg*, the largest airship ever built, exploded while docking at Lakehurst (page 44). The accident, which took the lives of 35 people, was partly the result of using flammable hydrogen.

The German Air Ministry ordered that the *Graf Zeppelin* be grounded until helium could be obtained from the United States, which was the only source of the gas. But the United States, fearful of Adolph Hitler, who was expanding Germany's armed strength and beginning to act aggressively toward small European nations, refused to supply the vital gas.

Early in 1938, the *Graf Zeppelin* was scrapped, a dismal end for an airship that had won the greatest renown for its owners, brought pleasure to tens of thousands, and had been cheered by millions in almost every corner of the globe.

Other Data (LZ-127 *Graf Zeppelin*)
Length: 776 ft.
Diameter: 100 ft.
Gas Volume: 3,700,000 cu. ft.
Power Plant: Five 550-hp Maybach engines
Maximum Speed: 80 mph

On trips to the United States, this hangar at Lakehurst, New Jersey, was home to the *Graf Zeppelin*.

ZRS-4 *AKRON*

With the *Graf Zeppelin* and other airships, Germany's Zeppelin Company planned to establish transoceanic passenger service. That was the British plan, too. Two airships, the R-100 and R-101, were built in the late 1920s by the British to provide commercial passenger service between London and India.

In the United States, however, airships were expected to play a military role. So it had been with the *Shenandoah* and *Los Angeles*. So it was to be with the *Akron* and *Macon*, two rigids that the U.S. Navy asked the Goodyear Zeppelin Company to build in 1928.

The *Akron* and *Macon* were to be the biggest and fastest airships of their time. What also made them unique was their mission; they were meant to serve as flying aircraft carriers.

An aircraft hangar was built inside each of the airships. The hangar was the home for four F9C Sparrowhawks. This small aircraft, each with a wingspan of 25 feet and weighing 2,770 pounds, less than a modern-day family automobile, were scout planes. Their job was to range far and wide, collecting information about enemy sea or land forces. The information would be reported back to the mother ship.

Before construction began on either the *Akron* or *Macon*, a special hangar—or airdock—had to be built at the Akron (Ohio) airport to house the two airships. Once completed, the hangar ranked as one of the world's largest structures without interior support.

The *Akron* made its first flight on September 23, 1931. Its tragic end came less than two years later.

Completed framework of the *Akron*. Work of covering the frame with fabric has begun at the nose.

Still in use today as a manufacturing facility, the hangar is 1,175 feet long, 325 feet wide, and 211 feet high. Ten football games could be played under its roof at one time or six miles of railroad track could be laid on its 8½ acres of floor space. The hangar is so huge it generates its own weather system. Sometimes clouds form inside and it rains.

Construction of the *Akron* began in 1929 and was completed in 1931. The airship was designed from the beginning to be inflated with nonflammable helium. This enabled engineers to mount the airship's eight engines inside the hull without having to worry about a fire or an explosion. The control car was fixed to the underside of the airship's nose.

Artist's drawing shows relative size of (from top to bottom) the *Akron, Los Angeles,* an Army blimp of the 1920s, and the Navy's 95-foot "Pony Blimp," dating to 1921.

The *Akron* made its first flight on September 23, 1931. It carried 113 people. Commanding the airship was Lieutenant Commander Charles Rosendahl, a pioneer in the development of lighter-than-air craft, and one of the survivors of the *Shenandoah* disaster six years before. Later in 1931, the *Akron* made a ten-hour flight with 270 passengers, and thus established a record for the number of passengers carried by an airship.

In the *Akron* the Navy at last seemed to have the rigid airship it had long wanted, one that could play an active part in fleet operations. The old German-built *Los Angeles* was taken out of service in 1932. It was planned to have as many as ten *Akron*-class zeppelins on active duty with the Navy.

In fleet maneuvers, the *Akron* successfully demonstrated its ability to launch and recover the tiny Sparrowhawk. Each of the airplanes was fitted with a special "skyhook" mounted at the midpoint of the upper wing. Flying at exactly the same speed as the airship, the pilot of the Sparrowhawk would ease the hook onto the horizontal bar of a recovery trapeze that hung down from beneath the airship's belly.

Once the hookup had been completed, the pilot would cut the engine, and the plane would be raised into the airship's hangar.

To launch a Sparrowhawk, the process was reversed. While hanging from the trapeze, the plane would be lowered with its engine running, then released to become airborne. The *Akron* could launch and recover aircraft when surface weather conditions made it impossible for aircraft carriers to conduct air operations.

On one occasion, six Sparrowhawk pilots made 104 hook-ons and takeoffs from the *Akron* in the space of three hours. Pilots called such operations "belly-bumping."

Despite this and other achievements, not everyone had good things to say about the *Akron*. Many naval officers felt that the airship wouldn't last very long in combat. Its enormous size and the relatively slow speed at which it traveled

Akron's gigantic tail structure dwarfs spectators who have gathered to view the airship.

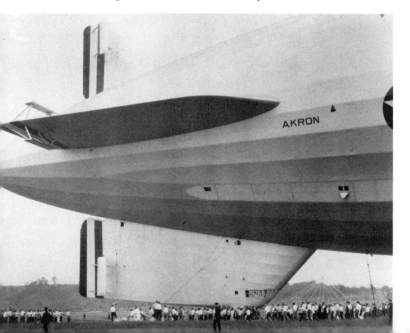

would make the *Akron* an inviting target for enemy fighter planes.

A series of unfortunate accidents gave ammunition to the airship's critics. A tail fin was severely damaged in a mooring accident. Later, two members of the *Akron's* ground crew failed to release the ends of the mooring lines they were holding when the airship suddenly rose in the air. They were carried to the height of 200 feet, and then dropped to their deaths.

There was no television in those days to replay the horrible accident. But there were newsreels. Cameramen had recorded the tragedy and the film was shown in the nation's movie theaters, horrifying millions.

The worst was yet to come. On April 4, 1933, when the *Akron* was eighteen months old, the airship flew into a turbulent storm off the coast of New Jersey.

Heavy rain pounded the airship. Lightning flashed in the sky. As the *Akron* pitched and rolled, the captain headed the ship out to sea in an effort to get away from the storm.

Not long after midnight, the *Akron* began falling rapidly. The ship leveled off, then dropped again. Its tail smashed into the sea and was ripped off by the impact. Then the ship's belly hit the water. Hammered by the water and wind, the airship broke up. Of the 76 men aboard the *Akron* , only three were saved. It was the worst accident in airship history.

Only surviving Sparrowhawk is on display at the National Air and Space Museum, Washington, D.C.

There is a footnote to this story. On July 31, 1986, a marine research team found the remains of the *Akron* about 40 miles off the New Jersey coast at Beach Haven. "It's right down there on the sea bottom, 105 feet down," said Jeff Loria, the director of the project. "There are pieces of metal frame ranging from 30 to 120 feet in length, crusted with marine life, and spread over a debris field about 700 feet in length." Material recovered from the *Akron* was to be turned over to the Navy.

Other Data (ZRS-4 *Akron*)
Length: 785 ft.
Diameter: 132.9 ft.
Gas Volume: 6,500,000 cu. ft.
Power Plant: Eight 560-hp Maybach engines
Maximum Speed: 83 mph

ZRS-5 *MACON*

Just three weeks after the tragedy that claimed the *Akron*, the *Macon*, sister ship to the *Akron*, made its first flight. The new ship was almost a perfect duplicate of the older one, except that it was about 8,000 pounds lighter. Like the *Akron*, the *Macon* had a hangar for storing four F9C Sparrowhawk scout planes.

The airship was named in honor of the largest city in the Georgia Congressional district of Carl Vinson. As chairman of the House Committee on Navy Affairs, Vinson was a very powerful figure in Washington.

The *Macon* was based at the new Naval Air Station at Sunnyvale, California, which had been named Moffett Field. Rear Admiral William A. Moffett, Chief of the Bureau of Aeronautics, had perished in the *Akron* disaster.

In 1933 and 1934, the *Macon* took part in combat exercises with the Pacific fleet. The airship crew spent much of its time perfecting the recovery and release of scout planes.

On a flight from California to the West Indies in the fall of 1934, the *Macon* was battered by fierce winds over the southwestern United States. These weakened the airship at those points where its tail fins joined the main hull structure.

Some repairs were made in the months that fol-

The *Macon,* sister ship to the *Akron,* was the last of the Navy's rigid airships.

lowed. But on February 12, 1935, when the *Macon* lifted off from Point Sur, California, on what was to be its 55th flight, there was still a weak point where the upper tail fin was connected to the hull.

The *Macon* was heading north along the California coast when the sky darkened. Rain drummed down on the airship and the wind turned blustery. Suddenly a vicious crosswind ripped away the airship's upper tail fin. Three gas cells were punctured as the fin was torn from the airship. As the gas leaked out, the airship dropped tail-first toward the water.

By dropping ballast and fuel, the captain was able to halt the *Macon's* descent. But as the helium continued to leak out, the ship started falling toward the sea again.

The captain saw that there was no chance to save the *Macon*. He ordered the engines stopped and began preparing for an emergency landing at sea.

The airship's tail hit the water first. Crew members leaped from the hull, then climbed into rubber life rafts and started paddling away from the airship as the sea closed over it.

Navy ships hurried to the area to pick up the survivors. Of the 76 men on the last flight of the *Macon*, only two were lost.

The loss of the *Macon* signaled the end of the U.S. Navy's experiment with rigid airships. Of the five that had been built for the Navy, four—the ZR-2, *Shenandoah*, *Akron*, and *Macon*—had destroyed themselves. Only the *Los Angeles* survived long enough to die of old age.

The American public thought that big rigid airships were very dangerous. Naval experts believed they were useless. With the loss of the *Macon*, an era ended.

Other Data (ZRS-5 *Macon*)
Length: 785 ft.
Diameter: 132.9 ft.
Gas Volume: 6,500,000 cu. ft.
Power Plant: Eight 560-hp Maybach engines
Maximum Speed: 83 mph

Four of the eight 560-hp Maybach engines that powered the *Macon*.

LZ-129 *HINDENBURG*

The *Graf Zeppelin's* enormous success as a passenger craft inspired Hugo Eckener to design a new, much bigger, and more powerful airship, one that would boast even greater comfort and safety. Construction on the new zeppelin, designated the LZ-129, began in 1934. But even before construction started, it was decided to name the ship the *Hindenburg* to honor Field Marshall Paul von Hindenburg, the much-admired German war hero who had become Germany's president in 1925.

The *Hindenburg*, 804 feet in length, 28 feet longer than the *Graf Zeppelin*, was the biggest airship ever built. It was longer than two football fields plus two tennis courts laid end-to-end.

The *Hindenburg* had a gas capacity of more than 7,000,000 cubic feet, almost double the *Graf's* volume. The gas the airship was designed to use was helium. But the United States, which had a monopoly on helium, would not sell the precious gas to Germany. Adolph Hitler had come to power in Germany, and war clouds were beginning to gather over Europe. The U.S. had no intention of releasing helium to a Germany led by Hitler.

The Zeppelin Company had no choice but to fill the *Hindenburg* with hydrogen—and try to make the airship as safe as possible. Passengers had their matches and lighters taken away from

"Two days to cross the ocean," boasts a poster hailing the *Hindenburg*.

If stood on end, the *Hindenburg*, at 805 feet, would have towered over 555-foot Washington Monument.

them as they came aboard. Crewmen who strode the catwalks between the 16 fabric cells that held the airship's hydrogen wore sneakers or shoes made of felt to prevent static electricity and the sparks that resulted from it.

Passengers who wanted to smoke could do so only in a special room which had been fully fireproofed. It was equipped with cigarette lighters that were chained down so they could not be carried to another—nonfireproof—part of the ship.

And the *Hindenburg's* four 1,200-horsepower engines were driven by crude oil that would not burn even, it was claimed, if a flaming match were tossed into the fuel tank. The *Graf Zeppelin's* engines ran on gasoline or gaseous fuel.

The *Hindenburg* began its career in passenger service in 1936, making six round trips between Germany and Rio de Janeiro in Brazil, and ten trips to the United States. It carried a total of 2,656 passengers on these voyages.

A one-way trip across the Atlantic to the United States cost $400. Passenger staterooms were quiet and comfortable. Each included a shower (although water was strictly rationed). Fine meals were served on blue and gold porcelain. A dozen stewards were on hand to pamper the passengers. One of the airship's most popular features was a 200-foot promenade deck that almost never failed to provide a spectacular view.

Passengers experienced little rolling or pitch-

Special stamps were issued to honor the *Hindenburg*. This postmark commemorates the airship's first flight to South America.

ing. On one voyage in 1936, young Nelson Rockefeller, later a vice president of the United States, is said to have asked one of the stewards: "When are we leaving?"

"Why, we left almost an hour ago," the steward replied.

The *Hindenburg* began its 1937 flight schedule in mid-March with a trip to Rio de Janeiro and return. When that was completed, the airship left Frankfurt, Germany, with 97 people aboard bound for Lakehurst, New Jersey.

In mid-afternoon on May 6, the *Hindenburg*

arrived over New York City. Although New Yorkers had seen the airship many times before, it still stirred wonder and excitement. From one end of the city to the other, faces turned up to watch. At 3:32 P.M., the great airship passed the Empire State Building and headed south for Lakehurst.

About a half an hour later, the *Hindenburg* was sighted by spectators who had gathered at Lakehurst. Captain Max Pruss, the *Hindenburg's* commanding officer, didn't like the look of dark clouds he saw as the ship approached, and he decided to delay the airship's descent until conditions became more favorable.

At 7:25 P.M., Pruss began bringing the airship in for its landing. When the *Hindenburg* was about 700 feet from its mooring mast, Pruss ordered the engines reversed. The ship's headway was quickly halted. Two trail ropes were dropped from the airship to be quickly taken by the ground crew. The ship hung in the air about 75 feet from the ground.

Suddenly a plume of flame burst from the top of the ship. Within seconds, a great mushroom of flame billowed above it. "My God, it's a fire!" a spectator shrieked.

Explosions racked the *Hindenburg* and the airship's structure began to crumble. The bow shot up and then the airship settled to the ground in a great mass of flame.

The *Hindenburg* soars over New York City on May 6, 1937, bound for Lakehurst, New Jersey, and tragic end.

Anyone who witnessed the disaster was filled with horror. Later, when newsreels of the tragedy were shown in theaters, the footage often produced screams from the audience.

Of the 97 people on board, 62 managed to escape with their lives. Captain Pruss was one of the survivors.

The captain and several crew members were convinced that the *Hindenburg* had been the victim of a bomb. But no evidence was ever produced to support that belief.

The official report on the disaster said that the hydrogen had probably escaped from a gas cell that had been damaged by a bracing wire. The escaping gas filled the space inside the upper fin. A discharge of static electricity had ignited it.

May 6, 1937, the date the *Hindenburg* exploded at its Lakehurst mast, signaled the end of the development and construction of rigid airships. Indeed, not a single rigid has flown a passenger since that date.

There was another factor—the airplane. By the mid-1930s, the airplane had become capable of safe, dependable, long-range flight. And planes were many times faster than airships.

In 1928, the year the *Graf Zeppelin* completed its first transatlantic crossing, U.S. international airlines carried 1,873 passengers. By 1937, the year the *Graf* was taken out of service, the number had increased almost tenfold, to 139,955. Even then, it was obvious—the future of commercial air transportation belonged to the airplane.

Other Data (LZ-129 *Hindenburg*)
Length: 804 ft.
Diameter: 135 ft.
Gas Volume: 7,063,000 cu. ft.
Power Plant: Four 1,200-hp Mercedes Benz diesel engines
Maximum Speed: 84.4 mph

In 34 seconds, the *Hindenburg* was reduced to a smoldering ruin.

LZ-130 *GRAF ZEPPELIN II*

The fiery destruction of the *Hindenburg* did not put an immediate end to the era of the rigid airship. It lingered on in the form of the LZ-130, a sister ship to the *Hindenburg*.

At the time of the *Hindenburg* explosion in 1937, the LZ-130 was under construction. Early the next year, as the airship neared completion, Hugo Eckener and the Zeppelin Company sought to buy helium from the United States to fill the LZ-130's fuel cells. A helium-inflated airship could win widespread public support in Germany, Eckener believed, wiping out memories of what had happened to the *Hindenburg*.

Franklin D. Roosevelt, then President of the United States, and many military leaders favored exporting enough helium to Germany to fill the airship. But in March, 1939, Adolph Hitler ordered German troops into Austria and seized the country. The move frightened other European nations. The continent appeared on the brink of war. The United States changed its mind about sending helium to Germany, believing that an airship filled with the vital gas could serve a military purpose.

Construction of the LZ-130 was completed in the fall of 1930. The ship was inflated with hydrogen and named the *Graf Zeppelin II*.

American fears that the LZ-130 might be used as a military weapon were fully realized. The airship was fitted out with an array of electronic detection equipment and flown on spying missions along the borders of Czechoslovakia, the

The era of rigid airships ended, not with the explosion of the *Hindenburg* in 1937, but with the scrapping of the LZ-130 three years later.

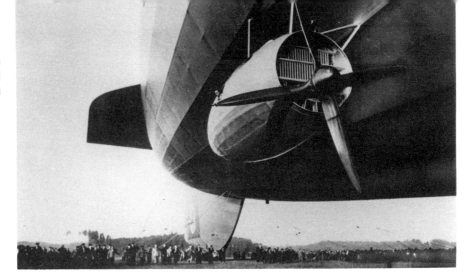

Opposite: One of the four 1,200-hp Mercedes Benz diesels that could drive the LZ-130 along at a speed a bit over 80 miles an hour.

Netherlands, Poland, and Great Britain. The airship's mission was to learn as much as possible about the radar defenses of those nations.

But Hitler and other of Germany's leaders believed that hydrogen-filled airships had no role to play in a shooting war. Virtually defenseless, they would be the easiest of targets for enemy fire, whether it came from the ground or the air.

In May, 1940, with German ground forces on the attack in Belgium, Luxembourg, and the Netherlands, Hermann Goering, chief of Germany's Air Force, ordered the destruction of both *Graf Zeppelins*. Many of the metal parts from the two airships went toward the construction of a German radar tower in the Netherlands. Zeppelin officers and crew members were shifted to other branches of the German armed forces.

After the war, little remained to remind anyone of the zeppelin era. The Zeppelin Company's construction sheds at Friedrichshafen had been flattened by American and British bombers.

Before long, air passengers would be traveling by jet planes, which had been developed during the war. A commercial jet could cross the Atlantic in a matter of hours. Like trolleycars or radio serials, zeppelins now seem a part of the distant past.

Other Data (LZ-130 *Graf Zeppelin II*)
Length: 804 ft.
Diameter: 135 ft.
Gas Volume: 7,063,000 cu. ft.
Power Plant: Four 1,200-hp Mercedes Benz diesel engines
Maximum Speed: 84.4 mph

K-SERIES

The tragic loss of the Navy's giant rigid airships—the *Shenandoah*, *Akron*, and *Macon*—seemed to spell the end of all airships, nonrigid as well as rigid. The fire that engulfed the German zeppelin *Hindenburg* in 1937 added to the bad name that airships had.

As a result, when World War II broke out in Europe in 1939, the U.S. Navy's Airship Service was practically nonexistent. While the base at Lakehurst, New Jersey, was still in operation, only a handful of nonrigids were to be found there and most of them seemed ready for the scrap heap. One was the ZMC-2, the old "Tin Balloon," the metal-clad airship that dated back to the 1920s (page 30).

However, Navy officials remembered the success they had enjoyed with nonrigids during World War I and the advantages that airships boasted when compared to heavier-than-air craft, to airplanes, that is. The biggest benefit that blimps offered was their range of speed—from zero to 75 miles an hour. This meant that an airship could easily protect not only the fastest ships in a convoy from submarine attack but also any vessel that happened to lag behind.

During the early months of 1940, the Navy

With a maximum speed of 75 miles an hour and the ability to range as much as 2,000 miles, K-class blimps played an important role in antisubmarine warfare during World World II.

Blimps sometimes put down on aircraft carriers to take on fuel and supplies.

began talking to the Goodyear Company about a fleet of modern airships. Out of these discussions came the K-class of nonrigid airships. These blimps were almost twice as big as the C-class blimps of 1918. In all, 135 K-class airships were built for the Navy by Goodyear during World War II.

Bases for the new airships were established at South Weymouth, Massachusetts; Weeksville, North Carolina; Sunnyvale and Santa Ana, California; and, of course, Lakehurst.

Because of their stability in the air, blimps made a perfect platform for the modern electronic instruments used in submarine detection — radar, sonar, and MAD.

Radar was used against any submarine that happened to be on the surface. Once a sub had been detected, the blimp would direct land-based aircraft or surface vessels to the kill.

Sonar (from **so**und **na**vigation and **r**anging) was used to seek out submerged submarines. Sonar equipment sent sound waves into the water.

When an outgoing sound wave struck an object under water, the waves rebounded. The echo, or "ping" as it was called, was then received back aboard the blimp. Sonar experts, by measuring the time it took the sound wave to rebound, could determine the distance between the object and their blimp.

The **magnetic airborne detector**—MAD—was also used for detecting submerged submarines. Developed from an instrument used in prospecting, MAD could locate large metal objects under

The U.S. Navy ordered 135 K-class blimps from Goodyear during World War II. Each carried an eight- or ten-man crew.

the surface. It worked like this: As the submarine cruised beneath the surface, it cut magnetic lines of force. The blimp above it could detect these changes with its MAD equipment.

"MAD-man contact!" the operator would call into the blimp's intercom system. Smoke floats and dye markers would then be dropped. The blimp would hover over the submarine as it called surface vessels or aircraft to the scene. The blimp also carried depth charges it could drop.

On at least one occasion, a blimp and a submarine became involved in a deadly "shoot-out." It happened during July, 1943, when the K-75, on patrol off the Florida coast, surprised a German sub cruising on the surface. The blimp slanted down to drop bombs and depth charges while members of its crew blazed away with machine guns. The U-boat answered back with its deck guns, and managed to tear a big gash in the airship's gasbag.

As the helium poured out, the blimp made a forced landing on the water. One of the airship's crew members was killed by a shark before rescuers arrived. The submarine fled. Later, the airship survivors had the satisfaction of learning that the U-boat had been found by surface ships and destroyed.

During 1943, airship cover was extended to include the Caribbean area. And in 1944, an airship fleet of six American blimps was assigned to patrol duties in European waters. On May 28,

1944, the six blimps left Weeksville and flew to Port Lyautey on the northern coast of Morocco, about fifty miles from the Strait of Gibraltar, where they were to patrol. When the airships arrived at Port Lyautey on June 1, it marked the first time the Atlantic had been crossed by a non-rigid airship.

The Navy's K-Series blimps built an impressive record during World War II. In fact, not one ship in a convoy escorted by a blimp was lost through enemy action during the war.

After World War II ended in 1945, the Navy quickly reduced the size of its airship fleet. All airship bases were put out of operation, except for Lakehurst. There would be blimps in the Navy's future but they would be cast in an entirely different role.

Other Data (K-14 - K-135)
Length: 251.7 ft.
Diameter: 62 ft.
Gas Volume: 425,000 cu. ft.
Power Plant: Two Pratt & Whitney 550-hp Wasp engines
Maximum Speed: 75 mph

After World War II ended in 1945, K-Series blimps were taken out of service. Their gasbags were deflated and put in storage.

ZPG-3W

The biggest nonrigids to be flown by the Navy were those of the ZPG-3W class. They were also the last.

Longer than a Boeing 747 airplane and about the size of an ocean-going liner in width, each ZPG-3W contained nearly seven times as much helium as one of today's GZ-20 Goodyear blimps (page 54). Each cost approximately $12,000,000 and carried a crew of 21.

The Navy ordered five ZPG-3Ws. The first flew in 1958.

The ZPG-3Ws were "early-warning" airships. Inside the envelope of each, revolving in the helium, was a radar scanner that was forty feet in diameter. The scanner's job was to detect any penetration of American airspace by enemy aircraft or missiles. With each circular sweep, the scanner covered an area that was approximately 400 miles in diameter.

The ZPG-3Ws were sometimes handed other missions. One of these resulted in a horrible tragedy. In July, 1960, a ZPG-3W based in Lakehurst, New Jersey, was assigned to search for two missing sea-going yachts. As the airship was carrying out its assignment, a long split developed in the blimp's envelope and the craft suddenly dropped from a windless sky into a calm sea. Eighteen men were trapped in the control car and drowned.

Soon after, the U.S. Navy brought its blimp

Blimps of the ZPG-3W series, 403 feet in length, 85 feet in diameter, were the biggest nonrigids ever flown by the U.S. Navy.

program to a close. The disaster that took place in July, 1960, is believed to have hastened the end of the program.

There were other and more important reasons, however. The last of the huge land-based radar stations that formed the nation's ballistic missile

A ZPG-3W blimp hooks up to a mooring mast at its Lakehurst, New Jersey, base.

early-warning chain had been completed. In addition, early-warning aircraft, such as Lockheed's WV-1 Warning Star and P-3 Orion, were in operation. These systems did the job that the ZPG-3Ws had been doing, and did it with greater efficiency.

On June 28, 1961, the Navy announced that it was ending airship operations. One by one the blimps were taken out of service and deflated.

In 1987, the U.S. Navy again began considering the use of blimps. Newer, faster, and more maneuverable than the ZPG-3Ws, the new blimps would house radar units and be used to detect the Soviet Union's sea-skimming missiles. "This is a case where twenty years later an old idea looks really good because of new technologies that help it overcome its problems," said Chuck Myers, a consultant for the Department of Defense.

In June, 1987, Westinghouse Airship Industries began working on an operational model of the new blimp. It was expected that the new airship would be flying early in the 1990s.

Other Data (ZPG-3W)
Length: 403 ft.
Diameter: 85 ft.
Gas Volume: 1,500,000 cu. ft.
Power Plant: Two 1,500-hp Curtiss-Wright
   engines
Maximum Speed: 80 mph.

GOODYEAR GZ-20

For over twenty years beginning in the mid-1960s, whenever the word blimp was mentioned, one immediately thought of Goodyear (the Goodyear Tire and Rubber Co.). The two went together like milk on morning cereal.

There were three blimps in the Goodyear fleet during most of those years. They were the *Enterprise, Columbia,* and *America.* (Goodyear named many of its blimps after racing yachts that had won the America's Cup.) One or another of the three blimps were seen by most Americans.

Each blimp traveled about 100,000 miles a year for Goodyear. They were in constant demand by the television networks for use as aerial camera platforms at major sports events. They appeared at the Rose Bowl and Orange Bowl football games, the Indianapolis 500 auto race, America's Cup yacht races, baseball's World Series, and pro football's Super Bowl.

The three blimps, each 192 feet in length and designated GZ-20, were based on a model that could be traced back as far as World War II. (The letters "GZ" stood for Goodyear-Zeppelin.)

Each of the GZ-20 blimps cost about $5.5 million to build. Operating expenses for the three amounted to approximately $10 million a year.

The blimp *Enterprise* spent six months a year at its winter base in Pompano Beach, Florida. The *Columbia,* based in Los Angeles, and the *Amer-*ica, operating out of Houston, had schedules that were similar to that of the *Enterprise.*

Between the years 1972 and 1987, Goodyear operated a fourth blimp in Europe. Named the *Europa,* it was also a GZ-20 ship.

Each of the three blimps operated in the United States carried approximately 8,000 passengers a year. That is a remarkable figure when one considers that only six passengers could be carried at a time.

The Goodyear blimp *Enterprise,* like others operated by the company, travels about 100,000 miles a year and is often used as an aerial platform for TV cameras.

Even more remarkable is the safety record achieved by the airships. In all their years of operation, Goodyear blimps have never had a passenger fatality.

A GZ-20 airship requires only a small amount of fuel. In fact, one could operate eight hours a day for almost a full week on the same amount of fuel a big commercial jet requires to taxi from its loading ramp to the runway for takeoff.

A feature of the blimp *Enterprise* was its "Super Skytacular" night sign on the sides of the envelope. After dark, the sign was used to flash public service announcements and Goodyear sales promotion messages to audiences below.

The sign on each side of the blimp was 105 feet long and 24.5 feet high. Each was made up of 3,780 lamps, or a total of 7,560 lamps on both sides. Eighty miles of wiring was used in connecting them. The sign could be read from a distance of one mile with the airship operating at an altitude of 1,000 feet.

Animated features could be programmed on the sign. These included a game of table tennis, a golfer driving his ball toward the green, and a

55

football player booting a field goal. At Fourth of July, one might see a youngster lighting a giant firecracker that exploded to form an American flag.

Blimp controls in a GZ-20 are manual. The pilot uses two foot pedals that are connected to cables to move the airship's two rudders back and forth. The rudders change the airship's direction from left to right, or vice versa.

A wheel mounted alongside the pilot's seat controls the elevators, which send the airship higher or lower.

Although a GZ-20 airship has no interior framework, it is not simply a balloon. Inside the helium-filled main envelope, or airbag, there are two smaller bags called ballonets. The ballonets are used to control the blimp's buoyancy and help maintain its shape.

As the airship gains altitude, the helium usually expands. This squeezes the air out of the ballonets.

When both ballonets are completely empty, the blimp is said to be at "pressure height." This is 10,000 feet in the case of the GZ-20.

When the blimp starts descending, the opposite happens—the change in pressure contracts the helium supply. Air is then driven into the ballonets to keep the airbag taut.

Riding in a blimp such as the GZ-20 is something like riding in a sea-going yacht. The

The airship *Enterprise* patrols the sky above its hangar home in Pompano Beach, Florida. Similar hangar in Houston, Texas, is home for the airship *America*.

airship rolls and pitches in the sky in much the same way a large boat does on the water's surface. There are none of the abrupt jerks or drops one feels in an airplane. In rough weather, however, you can get seasick in a blimp because of all the rocking and swaying.

Each of three GZ-20 Goodyear blimps was manned by a 22-man team. These included five pilots, mechanics, electronics experts, and a public relations representative. Not all are on duty at one time, of course.

The team was capable of operating the blimp anywhere in the United States, thanks to four specially equipped ground support vehicles. These moved from one city to the next in caravan fashion while the blimp flew overhead.

One of the vehicles was a big tractor trailer equipped to serve as a maintenance and repair facility. The unit included a machine shop and storage area for spare parts. It was also fitted with a mast to which the blimp could be tethered.

The support vehicles also included a bus equipped with a two-way aviation radio that served as a communications headquarters. A passenger van and a sedan for crew transportation were the other two vehicles that made up the caravan.

Between the years 1919 and 1987, Goodyear built 302 airships, more than any other company—or country—in the world. Of these, 244 were constructed for the U.S. armed forces, chiefly the Navy. When the last Navy blimp was retired in the early 1960s, Goodyear continued to build GZ-20 blimps for its own use. The *Enterprise, Columbia,* and *America* are the best-known examples.

Other Data (Goodyear GZ-20)
Length: 192 ft.
Diameter: 45.9 ft.
Gas Volume: 202,700 cu. ft.
Power Plant: Two 210-hp Continental engines
Maximum Speed: 50 mph

A scene from *Black Sunday,* a 1976 feature film. It's star: a Goodyear blimp.

SKYSHIP 500, SKYSHIP 600

From the mid-1960s through the mid-1980s, Goodyear's blue and silver blimps had the skies over the United States pretty much to themselves. Not anymore. In recent years, the Goodyear ships have crossed paths with the green and white blimp promoting Fuji film and tape, the red and gold blimp blazoned with McDonald's golden arches, and several others.

The Fuji blimp is fairly typical of the new airship crop. It's a Skyship 500, a blimp with a French-built envelope, a British-built cabin, and German engines, and one of a number operated in the United States by Airship Industries.

During the summers of 1986 and 1987, the Fuji blimp was often seen hovering over major league baseball parks. That's because the Fuji airship was the official videotaping sky platform for major league baseball.

Carrying a crew of ten, the Fuji blimp was fitted out with three camera booms and an on-board computer to help point both the airship and the camera electronically. The airship's twin Porsche

During 1986 and 1987, this Skyship 500 blimp served as the official videotaping sky platform for major league baseball.

6-cylinder turboprop engines were regarded as the most fuel efficient in the airship business. While the Fuji craft could soar as high as 10,000 feet, it usually operated at 1,000 to 5,000 feet.

Airship Industries also operates a bigger and slightly faster blimp in the Skyship 600. It has a top speed of 65 miles per hour (compared to 60 miles per hour for the Skyship 500).

During 1987, a Skyship 600 was leased to Pepsico, Inc., for a fee of $300,000 a month. Pepsico then adorned the airship with advertising for Slice, its new line of soft drinks.

In January, 1987, the Slice blimp took over for the Goodyear blimp in toting the television cameras used in aerial coverage of the Super Bowl. For all twenty previous Super Bowls, a Goodyear blimp had performed that chore.

The Slice airship was equipped with a special high-magnification camera that enabled television viewers to see close-up details of the game,

Flight deck of a Skyship 500 airship operated by Fuji Film. Controls are manned by pilot (left) and copilot.

even the numbers on players' jerseys. Previous blimp coverage had been limited to what were called "beauty shots."

Later in 1987, Airship Industries began using the Slice blimp for one-hour "Skycruises" over San Francisco Bay. Traveling at speeds of 30 to 60 miles an hour at an altitude of about 800 feet above the Bay, the blimp offered passengers breathtaking views of San Francisco's shoreline and a tower-height tour of the Golden Gate Bridge. The cost: $150 for a one-hour cruise.

The blimps operated by Airship Industries in the United States are based in Weeksville, a small coastal city in North Carolina not far south of Norfolk, Virginia. The 200-foot-high hangars and other facilities available there were used by the Navy airships during and in the years following World War II.

Weeksville is headquarters for the blimp pilots employed by Airship Industries. In 1987, the company had seventeen pilots, plus five in training. (Goodyear employed about twenty pilots at the time.)

To become a blimp pilot, one first has to be certified as a pilot for fixed-wing, multi-engine aircraft. Then the candidate receives at least twenty-five hours of flight training as a blimp copilot. That's followed by several months of work as a copilot before the candidate begins to tackle the 150 hours of flying time necessary in order to be eligible for a captain's wings.

"From a pilot's point of view, airships are very satisfying to fly," says Peter Buckley, chief pilot for Airship Industries. "It's not difficult, but it is demanding."

A blimp, says Buckley, is "pendulously stable" in the air. "You can feel it turn, twitch, surge, as if you're riding the waves."

The blimps representing Airship Industries and Goodyear were joined in the sky in 1985 by a 193-foot West German airship that came to the United States flying the colors of the McDonald's hamburger chain. With an airbag of 211,288 cubic feet and twin Rolls Royce Continental engines, "McBlimp," as it was called, cruised at 35 miles an hour but could zip along at 60 miles per hour with the aid of a favorable wind.

McBlimp and three of the airships operated by Airship Industries were brought together on July 5, 1986, for the "Great Blimp Race." Staged by the New York *Daily News*, the race was part of the weekend festivities celebrating the one-hundredth birthday of the Statue of Liberty.

The four blimps were to compete over a twelve-mile course that stretched from the George Washington Bridge down the Hudson River to the finish line in Battery Park. Most observers agreed the race was not very exciting. Blimps just don't look like they're racing. They just lumber along. (Airship Fuji won, averaging 46 miles an hour.)

What was exciting, however, was to see so many blimps in the sky at one time. Four blimps took part. The *Daily News* operated a camera blimp. And a Goodyear GZ-20 blimp, while not entered in the race, was also on hand. That's six blimps. It was hailed as the biggest gathering of blimps in almost half a century.

Other Data (Skyship 500)
Length: 164 ft.
Diameter: 46 ft.
Gas Volume: 160,000 cu. ft.
Power Plant: Two 205-hp Porsche engines
Maximum Speed: 60 mph

Other Data (Skyship 600)
Length: 194 ft.
Diameter: 54 ft.
Gas Volume: 211,000 cu. ft.
Power Plant: Two 250-hp Porsche engines
Maximum Speed: 55 mph

GOODYEAR GZ-22 *SPIRIT OF AKRON*

Called a "super blimp" by Goodyear, the GZ-22 is today's largest airship. Its 205½-foot-long envelope holds 247,800 cubic feet of helium. This makes the GZ-22 11½ feet longer and 36,800 cubic feet larger than its nearest rival.

The GZ-22 was christened and test flown in 1987. It went into full operation the following year.

The GZ-22 has the familiar shape of earlier Goodyear blimps. Its envelope is made of the same rugged, two-ply rubber-coated polyester fabric.

But the GZ-22 is the first airship to be powered by turbine engines—a pair of 420 hp Allison turboprops. The additional power these engines provide enables the GZ-22 to achieve a speed of 65 miles an hour. Maximum speed for GZ-22 blimps is 50 miles per hour. The GZ-22 is not only faster, it's quieter.

The GZ-22 carries nine passengers, plus its pilot. The older blimps carry only six passengers.

Instead of mechanical controls, that is, foot

Called a "super blimp," GZ-22 *Spirit of Akron* began operation in 1988.

pedals and a wheel to turn, the *Spirit of Akron* has a new "fly by wire" control system. In this, lightweight connections replace the mechanical hookups. These make the GZ-22 much easier to handle at low speeds.

Like the other Goodyear blimps, the GZ-22 goes on tour, transports guests, does public service promotion with its nighttime signs, and serves as a platform for network television cameras.

The GZ-22 is usually seen at altitudes of from 1,000 to 3,000 feet. It can operate as high as 10,000 feet, however. The ship's top speed is 65 miles an hour.

In naming the blimp the *Spirit of Akron*, Goodyear broke with the tradition of naming its airships in honor of America's Cup winners. The new blimp honors the city that has been a home for Goodyear since 1898.

Other Data (GZ-22 *Spirit of Akron*)
Length: 205.5 ft.
Diameter: 47 ft.
Gas Volume: 247,800 cu. ft.
Power Plant: Two 420-hp Allison turboprop
    engines
Maximum Speed: 65 mph

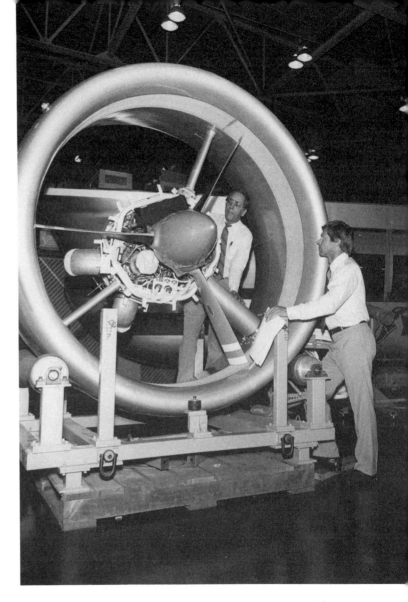

Engineers inspect one of the two 420-hp turboprop engines that power the *Spirit of Akron*.

AIRSHIPS ON EXHIBITION

Opened in 1976, the Smithsonian Institution's National Air and Space Museum in Washington, D.C., is well known for the dazzling array of flying machines and spacecraft it offers, everything from the Wright brothers' original 1903 *Flyer* to a Skylab Orbital Workshop. But in a gallery devoted to lighter-than-air flight, the Museum also features exhibits that are related to many of the airships and blimps featured in this book.

These include the actual control cabin of the Goodyear airship *Pilgrim*, which went into operation in 1925. The *Pilgrim* was the first airship designed for inflation with helium.

Also on display, suspended from the Museum's ceiling, is the one remaining Curtiss F9C Sparrowhawk. Eight of the tiny Sparrowhawks were assigned to the Navy's great airships, the *Akron* and *Macon*, as scout planes.

Several exhibits feature the *Hindenburg*. These include an enormous model of the airship and a special film prepared from footage that traces the *Hindenburg's* last flight. The airship is seen as it cruises majestically over New York City on its way to Lakehurst, New Jersey, where its final horrifying minutes are recorded. A coffee cup and a saucer, the cup bearing the seal of the company that operated the airship, were among the artifacts recovered from the wreckage. These, too, are on display.

More than ten million people visit the Air and Space Museum each year, making it the most popular museum in the world. The enormous cube-shaped structures that house the aircraft and exhibits stretch three city blocks, or 685 feet. (But, as one display demonstrates, the *Hindenburg* would have outstretched the Museum. At 804 feet, the airship was 119 feet longer than the Museum.)

The National Air and Space Museum is open every day of the year except Christmas Day. Write to the Museum (Independence Ave. between 4th and 7th Streets, S.W., Washington, D.C. 20560) for more information.

Airship models, artifacts, and photographs are also on display at these museums:

Naval Aviation Museum (Pensacola, FL 32508)

Pate Museum of Transportation (P.O. Box 711, Fort Worth, TX 76101)

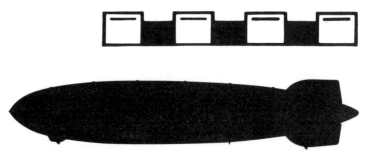

The National Air and Space Museum is big, but the *Hindenburg* was bigger.